D0118721

PASSPORT TO
FRANCE

Dominique Norbrook

Revised Edition

Franklin Watts

New York/Chicago/London/Toronto/Sydney

Copyright © 1985 Franklin Watts Limited
This edition 1994

Franklin Watts
95 Madison Avenue
New York, NY 10016

Library of Congress Cataloging-in-Publication Data
Norbrook, Dominique.
      Passport to France / Dominique Norbrook. – Rev. ed.
         p.   cm. – (Passport to)
      Includes index.
      ISBN 0-531-14293-0
      1. France – Juvenile literature.   [1. France.]   I. Title.
DD17.N67   1994   93-21188
944.083 – dc20   CIP AC

Design: Edward Kinsey
               Cooper-West
Illustrations: Hayward Art Group
Consultant: Keith Lye

Photographs: Chris Fairclough, J. Allan Cash,
Zefa, Denis Hughes-Gilbey, French Government
Tourist Office, Sporting Pictures, TFI, French
Railways, Robert Harding, Christian Dior,
Popperfoto, Renault, Moulinex, Airbus-Industrie,
The Mansell Collection, Phillips Collection.

Front cover: Eye Ubiquitous;
                  Hutchison Library (Bernard Regent)

Phototypeset by A. J. Latham Limited
Printed in Belgium

Contents

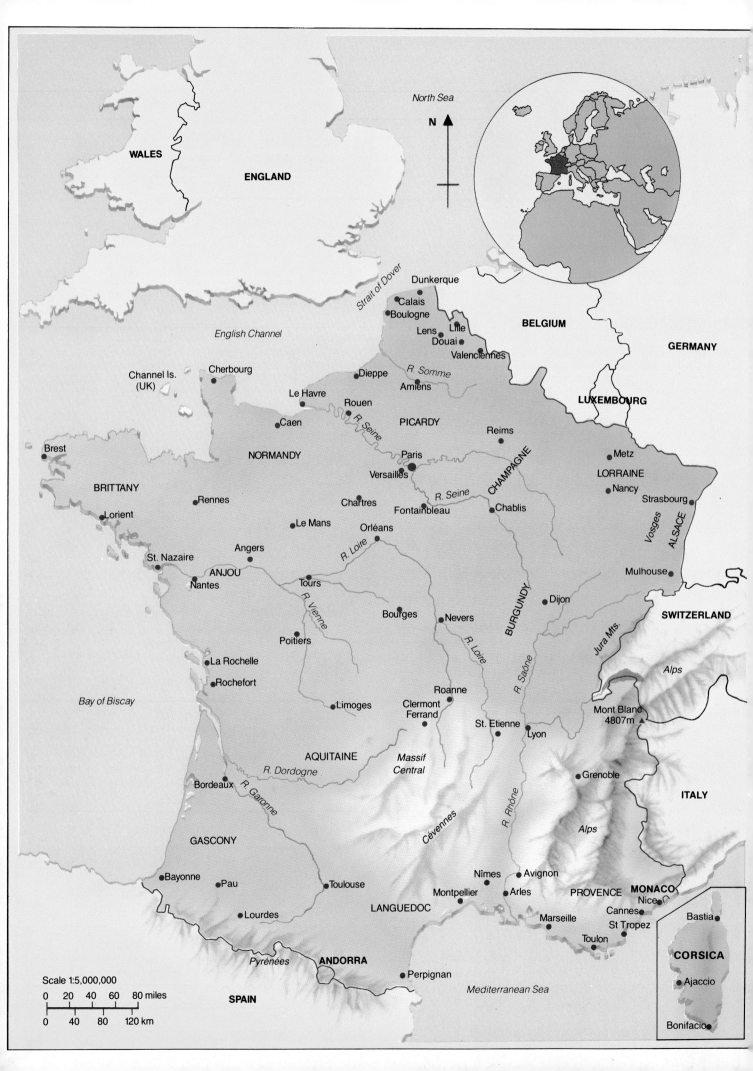

Introduction

France is an old and beautiful country in western Europe. Its official name is the French Republic. Except for Russia, it is the largest country in Europe. Metropolitan France includes the rugged Mediterranean island of Corsica, off the coast of Italy. France also has a number of overseas possessions, mostly small islands, in many different parts of the world.

As one of the world's leading industrial and agricultural nations, France is a rich country that plays a major part in world affairs. It is one of the five permanent members of the United Nations Security Council, a major partner in the European Economic Community (EEC), and takes the leading role among the world's French-speaking nations.

France is a land of contrasting scenery, in which peoples of different national origins have made their homes. Over the centuries the French have created a rich cultural heritage that has had a great influence throughout the world.

Above: French troops march proudly down the Champs Élysées, in the heart of Paris.

Below: A street in northern France shows the mixture of old and new that is France today.

The land

Within its 1,800-mile (3,000-km) coastline France contains some of the most varied scenery in Europe. It is a land of broad, fertile valleys, rolling plains, rugged mountains and long, sandy beaches.

France is often described as a country with six sides. Three sides are coasts. The others are borders with neighboring countries. The northwest coast faces the English Channel and is lined with sandy beaches, high cliffs, and busy ports such as Calais, Le Havre, and Cherbourg. At its western end the rocky coast of Brittany juts into the Atlantic Ocean.

The Bay of Biscay washes the shoreline of the west coast. The two main cities along this stretch are Nantes, on the Loire River, and Bordeaux, on the Garonne.

Southeastern France faces the Mediterranean Sea. West of the mouth of the Rhône River is a shoreline of beaches, lagoons, and saltwater marshes. To the east are the ports of Marseille and Toulon and the French Riviera, with its resorts of Nice, Cannes, and St. Tropez.

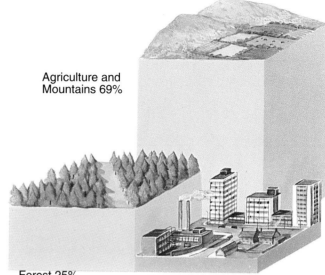

Agriculture and Mountains 69%

Forest 25%

Towns and Cities 6%

Above: France is able to make good use of its land area. Over three-fifths is suitable for agricultural use. Unusable land, such as mountains, cover quite a small area.

Below: Villefranche-sur-Mer is one of the many attractive seaside resorts along the French Mediterranean coast. It lies about 3 miles (5 km) from Nice.

More than two-thirds of France is less than 820 feet (250 m) above sea level. In the north is the Paris basin, a vast region of rich farmland drained by the rivers Seine, Loire, and Somme. In the southwest is the Aquitaine basin, another fertile agricultural region, through which runs the Garonne River. The valleys of the Rhône and Saône are two other important lowland areas that stretch from eastern France to the Mediterranean sea.

France's highest mountains are the French Alps and Jura Mountains, bordering Italy and Switzerland, and the Pyrénées, along the frontier with Spain. Mont Blanc, in the French Alps, rises to 15,771 feet (4,807 m) and is Europe's highest peak. The Massif Central, in southern France, is much lower but it covers nearly a sixth of the total area of the country and contains strange volcanic peaks and gorges. Other main upland areas include the Vosges Mountains, in the east, and the hills of Brittany, in the northwest.

Above: The rolling country of southern Burgundy, in central France, is known for the richness of its soils. It also offers perfect grazing land for herds of cattle.

Below: Mont Blanc towers above surrounding peaks in the French Alps. In the valley below is Chamonix, an important skiing resort and mountaineering base.

The people

The French are a complex mix of peoples. They are descendants of invaders and settlers who entered the country centuries ago. The earliest were Celtic peoples who arrived in about 1000 B.C. and called their new land Gaul. In 58 B.C. the Romans invaded Gaul and made it part of their great empire.

By the 5th century A.D. Roman power had declined and the country was invaded by Franks and other Germanic peoples from the east. About 400 years later Norsemen from Scandinavia settled in northern France and became known as the Normans.

Although France is now one nation, people in many parts of the country, notably the Basques and Bretons, still proudly preserve the separate national identities and languages of their ancestors of long ago.

In the 20th century many other foreign peoples have found a home in France. These include citizens of former French colonies and workers from Spain, Portugal, and Italy.

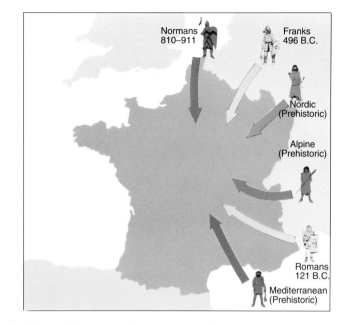

Normans 810–911

Franks 496 B.C.

Nordic (Prehistoric)

Alpine (Prehistoric)

Romans 121 B.C.

Mediterranean (Prehistoric)

Above: There were many prehistoric settlers in France before the invasion of peoples from other parts of Europe.

Below: The population includes people of many ethnic backgrounds. Many originally came from French colonies.

Above: Brigadier Chef Hothin, a policeman.

Below: Pierre Dewolf, a farmer.

Above: Mireille Infray, a restaurant owner.

Below: Gerard Desmedt, a journalist.

Although there is no such person as the "typical" Frenchman or Frenchwoman, French people do have certain characteristics in common. Both as individuals and as a nation the French like to be the best and first in everything. They like to think of themselves as different from other nations, with excellent taste in all things from furniture to food. French products are thought to be the best in the world.

They like order, but hate discipline if applied to themselves. So car drivers in a traffic jam often shout and wave their arms furiously at each other, each convinced the other is wrong.

French people rarely hold back their real feelings, and an evening with friends can often include fierce arguments. Despite this, the French admire a person who can reason things out logically, and they like cleverness and wit. They also like to criticize and laugh at each other. Complaining is an essential part of living, provided nothing changes too much!

Above: Chantal Larue-Bernard, a teacher.

Below: Jean Fefebure, a mailman.

Where people live

More than 56 million people live in France. But because these people are spread over such a large area, France is one of the least densely populated countries in Europe. There are only about 260 people per square mile (100 per square km) of land. In some parts it is possible to drive for hours without seeing a village or even a house.

Nearly eight out of ten people in France live in cities and towns. The largest numbers are concentrated in the big industrial and business areas, such as Paris, Lyon, and Lille, and in the many tourist resorts along the Mediterranean coast.

In recent years many people have moved out of the big cities to live in the pleasanter and cheaper surrounding districts. Others have left the old industrial regions of the north and east to work in newer industries in the warmer and sunnier south.

Above: Menton, on the Mediterranean coast, offers a pleasant and fashionable home.

Below: Saignon, in Provence, is a typical old village of this part of southern France.

Left: One of the modern housing developments close to Paris.

Below: Strasbourg, in Alsace, is an old cathedral city and river port. It has a strong Germanic influence as it is near the border of Germany.

Paris, with its "satellite" towns, is the largest urban area in Europe outside Russia. Many of its people live in modern housing developments in such new towns as Marne-la-Vallée.

In comparison with Paris, other French cities are only medium sized. There are only two cities, Marseille and Lyon, which, with their surrounding districts, have more than a million inhabitants, and three (Lille, Bordeaux, and Toulouse) with over half a million.

The provincial cities and towns cannot match the cultural attractions of Paris. But many contain outstanding historic buildings, notably medieval cathedrals. In these ancient towns old houses, lacking modern facilities, are often found alongside new developments.

Apart from television aerials and modern traffic, many small villages in rural areas throughout France still look the way they did centuries ago. Houses with shuttered windows face directly onto a main street, which often opens into a square enclosed by a church, small shops, and outdoor cafés.

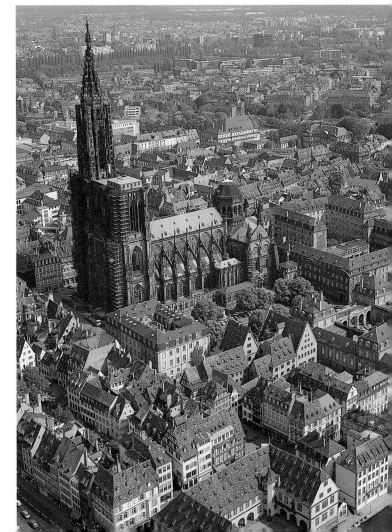

Paris

Paris, the capital of France, is the nation's government, business, and cultural heart. It is also one of the world's most beautiful cities, with elegant boulevards, spacious squares, and impressive buildings and monuments. There are also many fine hotels, shops, restaurants, and places of entertainment. Paris also has busy traffic, for it is a bustling, working city that lies in a major industrial region.

In area Paris is not a large city and only two million people live in the city itself. Nearly nine million people, however, live in the Greater Paris area.

The Seine River winds through Paris for about 8 miles (13 km), enclosed by high stone embankments and crossed by many bridges. The city spreads out on each side around the historic Ile de la Cité (City Isle). Here Paris was founded by Celtic peoples more than 2,000 years ago. As it grew, the city was encircled several times by walls. But these are long gone, and on their site there are now broad, tree-lined boulevards built in a grand plan between 1853 and 1870.

Above: The Eiffel Tower, a famous Paris landmark, dominates the city's skyline. It rises to a height of 1,056 ft (320 m).

Below: Some of the most popular sights to visit in Paris. Paris hosts many of the 30 million visitors every year to France.

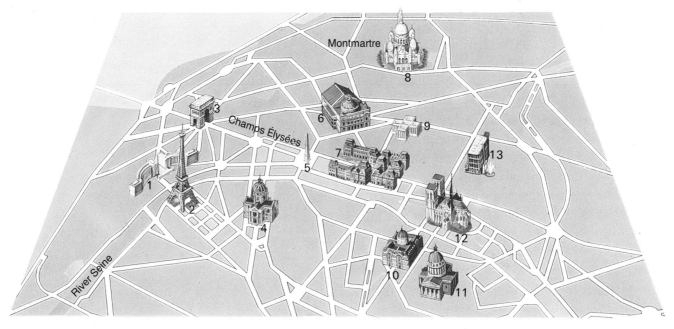

1 Chaillot Palace	5 Place de la Concord	9 The Bourse (Stock Exchange	12 Notre Dame
2 Eiffel Tower	6 Opera	10 Luxembourg Palace	13 Pompidou Center
3 Arc de Triomphe	7 The Louvre	11 Panthéon	
4 Invalides	8 Sacré-Cœur		

Several low hills rise above some parts of Paris. The highest, in Montmartre, reaches 426 feet (130 m). On it stands one of the city's best-known landmarks, the church of Sacré Cœur (Sacred Heart).

Many other places of interest are scattered around the city, most of them easily reached by the underground railway system, called the Métro. Among the most popular are the Eiffel Tower, the Louvre, the Tuileries Gardens, the Arc de Triomphe, and the Pompidou Center cultural complex. There are also such interesting sights as the richly ornamented Opera House and the Elysée Palace, the official residence of the French president.

Many people particularly enjoy the lively atmosphere of the Latin Quarter, the students' district on the left bank of the Seine. Others prefer the peaceful surroundings of the Luxembourg Gardens or the pleasant woods of the Bois de Boulogne.

Above: The Champs Élysées is the most famous of the boulevards that radiate from the Arc de Triomphe, in central Paris.

Below: The pleasant Tuileries Gardens occupy the site of a former royal palace near the Louvre Museum.

Fact file : land and population

Key facts

Location: France is on the western edge of the continent of Europe between latitudes 42° and 51° North.

Main parts: France contains twenty-two Metropolitan regions – twenty-one on the mainland and the island of Corsica. There are five Overseas Departments: Guadeloupe in the West Indies; French Guiana in South America; Martinique in the West Indies; Reunion in the Indian Ocean; and St. Pierre and Miquelon, a group of islands off the coast of Newfoundland, Canada.

Area: 211,208 sq miles (547,026 sq km), not including Overseas Departments.

Population: 56,342,000 (1990 census).

Capital: Paris

Major cities:
Paris (city, 2,189,000; city and suburbs, 8,707,000).
Other leading cities (with their city and suburb populations):
Lyon (1,221,000)
Lille (1,000,000)
Marseille (900,000)
Bordeaux (640,000)
Toulouse (541,000)
Nantes (465,000)
Nice (449,000)

Main languages: French (official). Other languages include Alsatian, a form of German (Alsace region), Basque (in the southwest), Breton (in Brittany); Catalan (western end of Mediterranean coast); and Provençal (southeast).

Highest point: Mont Blanc in the French Alps, 5,771 ft (4,807 m).

Longest rivers:
Loire, 628 miles (1,010 km)
Rhône, 503 miles (810 km)
Seine, 478 miles (770 km)
Garonne, 404 miles (650 km)

Largest lake:
Lac du Bourget, east of Lyon, 16.6 sq miles (43 sq km).

France has four main climatic types: *temperate marine*, near the northern and western coasts; *continental*, in central areas; *mountains*; and *Mediterranean*, near the southern coasts.

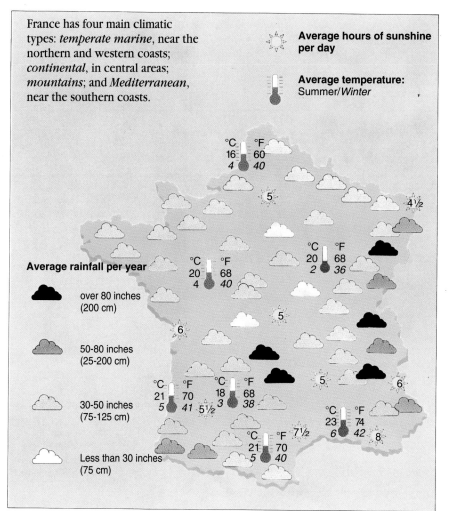

Average hours of sunshine per day

Average temperature: Summer/*Winter*

Average rainfall per year

over 80 inches (200 cm)

50-80 inches (25-200 cm)

30-50 inches (75-125 cm)

Less than 30 inches (75 cm)

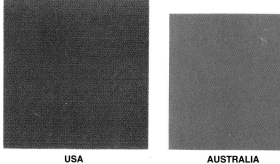

USA

AUSTRALIA

FRANCE   GREAT BRITAIN

△ **A land area comparison**
France's 211,208 sq miles (547,026 sq km) of land is small compared to that of countries such as the U.S. with 3,600,000 sq miles (9,370,000 sq km) and Australia with 2,470,000 sq miles (7,650,000 sq km). In European terms France is a large country. The United Kingdom, for example, has only 88,759 sq miles (229,979 sq km) of land. France has roughly the same land area as the United Kingdom, the former West Germany, Belgium, and the Netherlands all put together. Its coastline is 2,129 miles (3,427 km) including 400 miles (644 km) of Corsica.

Australia 5 per sq mile
(2 per sq km)

USA 70 per sq mile
(27 per sq km)

France 269 per sq mile
(105 per sq km)

Britain 614 per sq mile
(237 per sq km)

△ **A population density comparison**
France has a medium density of
population in world terms. France is
only one-third as densely populated as
some European countries.

Cities and towns
74%

Country 26%

△ **Where people live**
France is a highly urbanized
country. But in recent times the
increase of town and city dwellers
has slowed.

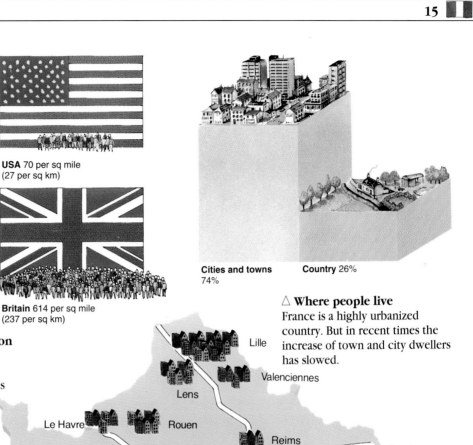

Major cities

Major routeways

Lille
Valenciennes
Lens
Le Havre
Rouen
Reims
Paris
Strasbourg
Brest
Le Mans
Nancy
Mulhouse
Dijon
Nantes
Tours
Lyon
Clermont Ferrand
St Etienne
Grenoble
Bordeaux
Nice
Montpellier
Marseille
Toulouse
Cannes
Toulon

△ **Major population centers**
The large cities of France are
generally located near the
coasts and along the inland
waterway systems.

Home life

Family life is highly valued in France. Traditionally, the home contained several generations—grandparents, parents and children. But in recent years families have become smaller. Three-fifths of them now have only two or three children. Also many children now leave home when they marry, although most live less than 12 miles (20 km) from their parents' homes.

Family ties often remain strong. Students usually go to local universities. Holidays, anniversaries, and birthdays are times for family reunions.

Most French people in urban areas live in apartments, which are usually rented. Many people have homes only a short distance from their place of work. Most people like modern homes which are easy to heat and clean. But they also like antique furniture, even though it may not be so comfortable.

Above: Bernadette and Guy Scoarnec live in Ivry, near Paris. Guy is an architect and Bernadette is taking a university course. They are seen in front of their home.

Right: The Scoarnec family sitting room is plain yet fashionable.

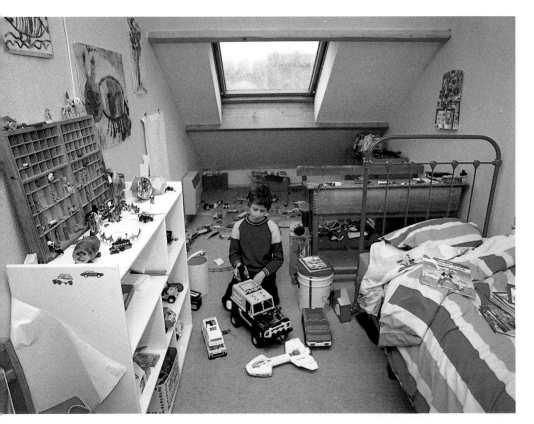

Below: Bernadette Scoarnec notes down shopping requirements for the next day.

The French are a hardworking people and many work long hours of overtime in order to earn more money. The average working week in 1990 was thirty-nine hours. About two out of every three women go out to work, mainly in service industries. While at work, they may leave their younger children in nurseries, which are partly paid for by the government.

There is not much time for leisure at the end of a working day. After the evening meal most people stay home and watch television, listen to the radio, or read the newspapers or a book. Some enjoy playing cards at home, while others like to go to the local café to meet friends and talk. Children usually have a lot of homework to do each evening during the week and many are not allowed to watch television before finishing it.

Since the 1960s many working people have had more time for leisure on weekends, because the factories now close on Saturday mornings. Nearly a third of all French people now spend some time gardening. Home improvements and cooking have also become popular pastimes for many people.

Shops and shopping

The French are very demanding shoppers who like to choose their goods with care. They would never hesitate to return a rotten apple or any other imperfect item to the shopkeeper. They know the best shops follow the motto "The customer is king."

Nearly all French towns have a market. French people love elbowing their way around the stalls looking for the best buys. The stalls sell almost every kind of food, cheap clothes, and all sorts of household articles. Larger towns often have specialized markets that sell only flowers, for example. Paris has a flea market where a great variety of old household articles can be bought. Markets are held every morning or perhaps twice a week, depending on the size of town.

At village markets local farmers often sell their own produce directly to customers from their trucks. For example, they sell fresh cheese, dairy products, honey, and eggs. Village markets are held only once or twice a week. Market day is an exciting event, and the streets and cafés become crowded.

Above and **below left:** Markets are a traditional and still important part of French shopping.

Below: Some of the many types of French bread. Most people buy their bread fresh each day from the local baker.

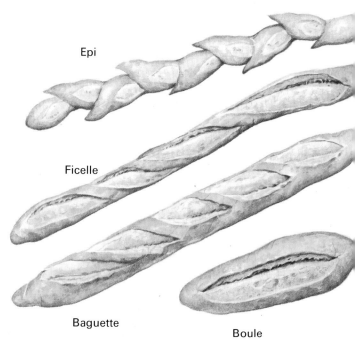

Epi

Ficelle

Baguette

Boule

Many people, particularly the elderly, prefer small local shops. Most of these have been run for many years by the same families, who get to know their customers personally. Shoppers enjoy a friendly chat while making their purchases.

France has a large number of small shops that specialize in one kind of product. These include the *boulangerie* (bread), *boucherie* (meat), *charcuterie* (cooked meats and sausages), and *épicerie* (groceries). Most small shops are closed between noon and 2 P.M., but stay open until 7 or 8 in the evening.

Many people prefer to shop in the big supermarkets and even bigger hypermarkets often found on the outskirts of towns. Here they can find everything, from a loaf of bread to household furniture. The goods are cheap and generally of high quality. All these markets have big car parks and many are open from about 10 in the morning until 10 at night.

Above: A *charcuterie* offers a tempting variety of cold meats, ready-prepared dishes, and many types of sausages.

Below: The French welcome the convenience of packaged food and few now insist that all food should be freshly prepared.

Cooking and eating

The French love good food and especially enjoy talking about it. For them, cooking is an art that greatly adds to their enjoyment of life. French *cuisine*, or cooking, is famous throughout the world. There are two main types—*haute cuisine*, which uses only the finest ingredients prepared by master chefs, and *provincal*, the traditional cooking of the regions.

Although meals in French restaurants may need a lot of elaborate preparation, everyday cooking at home is quick, simple, and tasty. A meal may consist of several courses, eaten with slices of fresh, crusty bread and accompanied by wine.

For the main course, cuts of meat, such as steaks or chops, may be fried with garlic and sprinkled with parsley or mixed herbs. Vegetables are served as a separate course. They are first lightly cooked and then perhaps fried with bacon and onions or sprinkled with cheese and baked in the oven. After the main course may come a fresh green salad or a selection of cheeses, followed by fruit or a dessert.

Above: The Scoarnecs' kitchen is compact with the most modern equipment.

Below: The Scoarnec family sits down to a simple meal of fresh salad and a selection of cheeses.

Mealtime is a special occasion for French people. They like to gather around the table as a family to chat as well as to eat. Breakfast generally consists only of *café noir* (black coffee) for the adults and *café au lait* (coffee with milk) for the children, with bread and jam. Pastry croissants are often eaten as a special treat for Sunday breakfast. For most families, lunch is the main meal of the day. Dinner, eaten at about 7 P.M., is a lighter meal.

Working people who cannot go home for lunch often prefer to eat a French-style sandwich in a café rather than a snack in a fast-food restaurant. French people sometimes like to dine in a restaurant with their family or friends on weekday evenings or Sunday lunchtimes, when they can take their time.

Restaurants in France generally welcome children of all ages, even if the chef has to make special courses for them. Then the dining room becomes more noisy and livelier than usual.

Above: Many restaurants are small family-run businesses that offer good food in simple surroundings.

Below: French chefs take great pride in their work and create their own specialities. A good chef is held in high regard.

Pastimes and sports

Soccer is by far the most popular sporting activity in France today, but traditional sports, such as shooting and fishing, are also enjoyed by millions of people. Tennis and riding, once the sports only of rich people, are growing rapidly in popularity, as are sailing and windsurfing.

In addition to people who like to take part in sports, there are also those who prefer to watch. Crowds of spectators flock to professional league soccer matches and games played by the French national team. Others attend rugby matches, including the annual international game for the "Triple Crown" between France, England, Scotland, Wales, and Ireland.

Another popular spectator sport is horse racing at such racetracks as Longchamps. Auto racing also draws large crowds for such famous events as the Le Mans 24-hour race, the Monte Carlo Rally and Grand Prix races. But perhaps the best-known event of all is the Tour de France cycle race, held since 1903, which tests the endurance of even the fittest riders.

Above: Boules is a traditional French game played with metal balls on any suitable patch of gravel or reasonably flat surface.

Below: Bicycle races are a major attraction. The Tour de France covers 2,500 miles (4,000 km) through the major regions of France over a three-week period.

Left: Les Ménuires is one of the many busy ski resorts in the French Alps.

Below: Windsurfing has become very popular at many southern French resorts. This is Cassis, on the Mediterranean coast.

Many French people particularly like sporting vacations and enjoy skiing and other winter sports in the mountains. In the summer months the mountains are also popular with climbers and hikers, and the country's many fine camping sites are generally crowded.

French people can pursue such outdoor activities more easily today, partly because they now have the right to five weeks' annual vacations with pay. As a result, people are taking several breaks at different times of the year to follow many different interests instead of just spending the traditional month's holiday at the beach.

The mass exodus of people in August from the towns to seaside resorts, however, still continues. The roads to the south are clogged with traffic and the beaches are crowded. The government is promoting many schemes to avoid the loss of production in August and the pressure on the resorts.

Cultural holidays exploring the history, arts, and crafts of France have recently grown in popularity. Regional tourist boards are also active in the promotion of special events in their areas.

News and broadcasting

France has a very sophisticated public broadcasting system and a dynamic publishing industry. Nearly half of all French people read a newspaper every day. Ninety-six daily newspapers are published throughout France, fourteen of them in Paris. The top sellers are *France-Soir, Le Monde,* and *Le Figaro* among the Paris dailies, and *Ouest-France, La Progrès* (Lyon), and *Sud-Ouest* among the regional newspapers. Nearly seven million of the 9.2 million newspapers sold each day are published in the regions of France.

Weekly newsmagazines, such as the top-selling *Paris-Match, L'Express,* and *Le Nouvel Observateur* are becoming increasingly popular. Also gaining in readership are technical and economic journals and specialist magazines on leisure interests, sports, and home improvement. But the weekly radio and television magazines sell most copies. French people buy about three million copies of *Télé 7 Jours* every week.

Above: National daily newspapers play an influential role in communication and opinion-making.

Left: News and current affairs are a favorite topic of conversation and discussion in the French café. Many people read the morning paper there, while having breakfast.

Left: Weekly magazines provide a pictorial insight into French and world events. Fashion is a very popular interest.

Above: A wide range of magazines and comics for the young are available. Astérix, a comic-strip character, is particularly popular.

The French also enjoy reading books, and book publishing is a major industry. Every year about 26,000 books are published, and over 360 million copies are printed. About a third of these are paperbacks, including detective stories and spy thrillers. Each title sells for the same price, whether it is bought in a bookshop or large store, or through a book club or mail order firm.

French people spend an average of thirty-two hours a week watching television and listening to the radio. The public television service provides three channels: TF1, Antenne 2, and FR3. There is also a private fourth channel, Canal Plus, which mostly shows films.

Radio programs are broadcast by the national corporation (Radio-France) and by local stations throughout France. Listeners can also tune in to French-language programs broadcast by Radio Luxembourg, Radio Monte Carlo, Europe 1 (from the Saar), Sud Radio (from Andorra), and other foreign stations.

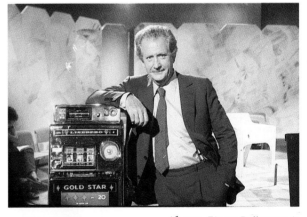

Above: Pierre Bellemare is a popular television game show host.

Left: *Télé 7 Jours* lists what is going to be shown on television during the coming week. A typical day's viewing presents a mixture of French and imported programs.

Fact file : home life and leisure

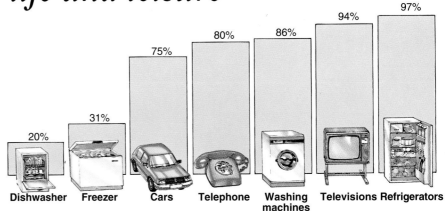

Dishwasher	Freezer	Cars	Telephone	Washing machines	Televisions	Refrigerators
20%	31%	75%	80%	86%	94%	97%

Key Facts

Population composition: In 1990 people under fifteen years of age made up 20.1 percent of the population; people between fifteen and sixty-four made up 66.1 percent; and people over sixty-five years made up 13.8 percent.

Average life expectancy: 72.7 years (1990), as compared with 72 years in 1970. Women make up 51.3 percent of the population of France, as compared with 48.7 percent men. This is because the average life expectancy for women is 81-9 years more than for men.

Rate of population increase: 0.5 percent per year in 1980-88, as compared with 1.1 percent a year in 1960-70.

Family life: The marriage rate in 1991 was 4.9 per 1,000 people. The average number of people in a household was 2.7. In the late 1980s, 60 percent of French people took their vacations away from home, for an average of thirty days a year.

Homes: 50.7 percent of French people own their main homes and about 54 percent of these homeowners live in houses, as opposed to apartments.

Work: In 1982, the statutory working week was reduced from forty hours to thirty-nine hours. The workforce in 1987 was 24,608,800. At the start of 1988, there were over 2 million job seekers. This was about 10 percent of the workforce.

Prices: Prices rose by 8.0 percent per year in 1965-80 and by 7.1 percent a year between 1980 and 1988.

Religions: The government does not officially recognize any church, but the largest is the Roman Catholic Church, which had an estimated 42.35 million members in 1986, though less than one-fifth were regular church attenders. In 1993, Protestants numbered about 850,000, and there were also about 1.9 million Muslims.

Leisure and arts	6.5%
Clothing and footwear	6.6%
Household goods and services	9.3%
Health	12.8%
Other goods and services	13%
Transport and communications	13.6%
Housing	17%
Food and drink	21.2%

△ **How many households owned goods in the early 1990s**
Many French homes have acquired new types of household goods in recent years. The biggest increase has been in television sets, ownership of which rose from 10 percent to 90 percent in 20 years.

◁ **How the average household budget was spent in the 1980s**
The proportion spent on food dropped from 36 percent in 1958 to about one-fifth in the 1980s. Increases have been seen in spending on housing, health, transportation, and leisure items.

▽ **French currency and stamps**
The French currency, the franc, is divided into 100 centimes. In 1989 there were about 5.6 francs to the U.S. dollar.

▽ **How the average family spends a working day**

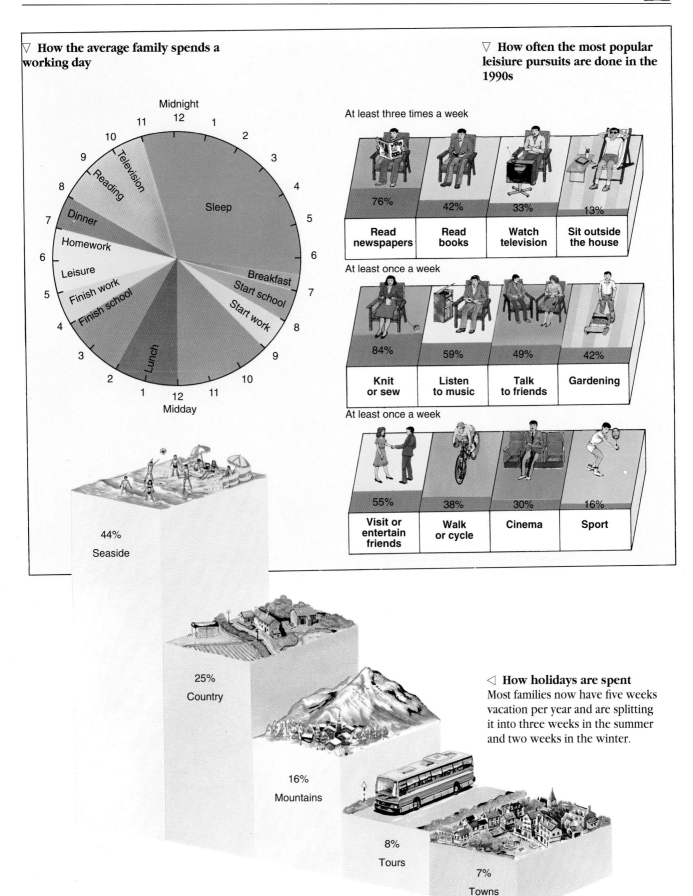

▽ **How often the most popular leisiure pursuits are done in the 1990s**

At least three times a week

76%	42%	33%	13%
Read newspapers	**Read books**	**Watch television**	**Sit outside the house**

At least once a week

84%	59%	49%	42%
Knit or sew	**Listen to music**	**Talk to friends**	**Gardening**

At least once a week

55%	38%	30%	16%
Visit or entertain friends	**Walk or cycle**	**Cinema**	**Sport**

44%
Seaside

25%
Country

16%
Mountains

8%
Tours

7%
Towns

◁ **How holidays are spent**
Most families now have five weeks vacation per year and are splitting it into three weeks in the summer and two weeks in the winter.

Farming and fishing

France is one of the world's most important agricultural countries. French farms are Western Europe's leading producers of beef, veal, poultry, and cheese. They also produce large quantities of milk, eggs, sugar, and grain crops, including barley and wheat.

More than three hundred kinds of cheese are made in France, using milk from cows, ewes, and goats. Among the best known are Camembert, Brie, and Roquefort, which are exported to most countries of the world.

Cattle are raised mainly in the northern and western regions of the country, particularly Brittany. Grain crops are grown in the vast open fields of the north, especially around Paris. Fruit and vegetables come from Brittany and the warmer parts of the south. Sheep and goats are herded in the mountainous southern and eastern regions, while pigs and poultry are kept on farms all over the country.

In the past French farms were mostly very small. But during the last thirty years French agriculture has been greatly modernized to create larger and more efficient farms using fewer workers.

Above: A farmer working on a small-holding in Brittany.

Below left: A selection of the vast range of French cheeses. Nearly every village makes it own type.

Below: Some of the main breeds of French cattle. Each is named after the region where it was first raised. French breeds have been exported to many other countries due to their fine reputation.

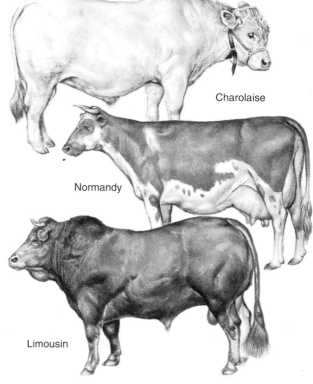

Charolaise

Normandy

Limousin

Above: Each wine-growing region has a different shape of bottle.
Left: Harvesting grapes by hand near Beaune, the wine capital of Burgundy. Machines are increasingly being used for this work.

Below: Unloading a fishing boat at La Turballe in Brittany. The French fishing ports on the Atlantic and Channel coasts account for over three-quarters of the French fishing catch.

Many of the changes in French farming are a result of the Common Agricultural Policy (CAP) created by the Common Market (EEC). Unfortunately, this has also encouraged farmers to produce too much of some kinds of products, particularly butter, milk and wine.

France is famous for its excellent wines. Large quantities of high-quality wines are exported to all parts of the world. Among them are such well-known names as Champagne, Burgundy, Bordeaux, Beaujolais, and Sauterne. Because of overproduction of cheaper wines in recent years, the French government has encouraged the making of better-quality wines.

The timber industry is being promoted by the government in anticipation of a timber shortage in Europe.

The fishing industry until recently was in decline but increased investment in ships and new technology is now being made.

Natural resources and industry

France is one of the world's most important industrial nations. From its factories come such well-known French products as automobiles, aircraft, computers, and spacecraft. France also has many small traditional craft industries including pottery and textiles.

The main industrial regions of France include the areas around Paris, Lille, and Lyon and in Lorraine. There are also newer areas in various parts of the country where high-technology industries have developed in recent years.

France is not rich in natural resources, although it does have deposits of coal, iron ore, bauxite, and other minerals. Because it produces little oil, an increasing part of the electricity needed to run the factories is now generated by nuclear power stations in various parts of the country. Research is also being done into new energy sources. A solar power plant has been in operation in the Pyrénées since 1970 and another is planned.

Below: A production line at Renault, France's largest car-making company.

Above: Large deposits of iron ore, bauxite, and coal are mined in France.

Above: The symbols of France's leading car makers.

About a quarter of French working people are employed in industry. Many work in the steel industry, which developed using French ores. In the same way, the mining of bauxite created the important aluminum industry. Much of the metal produced by these industries goes to make automobiles in the factories of such large companies as Renault and Peugeot-Talbot-Citroën. It is also used by many other companies to make industrial machinery and equipment and household items such as washing machines and refrigerators.

The French chemical industry employs about two million people in factories that make a wide range of products. It is Europe's leading maker of fertilizers and is also one of the world's leading exporters of tires and glass products.

Exciting progress has been made in recent years in the development of electronics industries in France. Their products include computers, robots, telecommunications equipment, and space technology. The French aircraft industry has played a leading role in the production of the supersonic airliner Concorde and recently of the European Airbus airliner. France is also a leading armaments manufacturer.

Above: The Airbus A-300, first flown in 1974, was a joint venture by France, Spain, the former West Germany, and the United Kingdom. A new medium-haul airliner was introduced in 1988.

Below: Microwave ovens being assembled at Moulinex, the leading French maker of domestic appliances. The company's products are exported around the world.

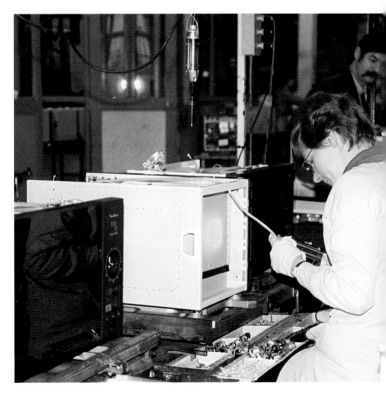

The perfume and fashion industry

Women throughout the western world have always admired the elegant clothes and beautiful perfumes worn by well-dressed French women. France is a world leader in the perfume and fashion businesses.

Perfume has been made in France since the sixteenth century. The fragrant flowers needed to make it were grown in the south of the country, where a busy industry developed. Today, fragrant plant oils and animal extracts used in making the perfumes come from all over the world. But because the natural ingredients are costly, perfume makers also use many synthetic fragrances made from chemicals, such as coal tar or petroleum. They can make a much wider and cheaper range of perfumes from these substances.

Perfume became a major business in the 1920s. The great fashion designers of Paris began to promote fragrances that carried their names, among them Worth and Chanel. More recently, Dior, Fath-Balmain, Cardin, Yves St. Laurent, and Guy Laroche have also become well known, and their products are exported all over the world.

Above: A lavender field near Grasse, in the south of France.

Left: Perfume research in progress in a factory in Grasse, where most French perfume is made.

Left: A new creation being fitted on a model at the famous Chanel boutique in Paris.

Above: Yves St. Laurent is one of the best-known French fashion designers.

Below: A new collection is presented.

Paris has been a fashion center since the fourteenth century but the modern industry was begun in the nineteenth century by an Englishman, Charles Frederick Worth. He founded the first couture, or fashion house, in 1858, with fashion shows, models, sales staff, and Paris labels. In the twentieth century a series of great designers continued the dominance of Paris.

Today, fashion remains one of France's best-known exports. Every year the great fashion houses of Paris hold seasonal shows to display their latest creations. Their designs often have a great influence on style around the world.

Since the 1960s French designers have also developed an immense trade in cheaper, ready-to-wear clothes and accessories.

The high reputation and success of the fashion business are today helping the French textile industry to survive stiff competition from other countries, where production is cheaper.

Transportation

France has a highly developed transportation system. By the late 1980s it had 5,337 miles (8,590 km) of highways, or *autoroutes*, with more under construction or planned. Drivers have to pay tolls to use these roads. There are also about 17,500 miles (28,200 km) of older highways called *routes nationales*. In the north these major roads radiate like a spider's web around Paris. To cross the country without going through the capital, drivers may have to use smaller roads.

Because France has few long-distance buses, many people travel on the efficient railway system, much of which is electrified. The railways have about 21,500 miles (34,600 km) of track. The National Society of French Railways (SNCF) provides modern, comfortable trains that run punctually. The boring of the Channel Tunnel, linking France and Britain, began in 1988.

All French cities provide generally cheap and reliable public bus services. In some larger cities, including Paris, Marseille, Lille, Lyon, and Toulouse, there are also underground railway networks.

Above: France has one of the most modern highway systems in the world. Over half of all freight goes by road.

Below left: The new high-speed train, the TGV.
Below: The Paris Métro, an underground railway system.

Above: Symbols of leading French transportation organizations: (top to bottom) Air France, the National Society of French Railways, and the Paris Public Transport Authority.

Above: Waterways play a major role in the transportation of freight for factories near Lille, in northern France.

Below: Dunkirk is a leading French port in northern France and handles both freight and passengers.

Navigable inland waterways are an important means of transporting freight such as farm produce, building materials, petroleum products, and mineral fuels. The waterways include the Rhone-Saône, Rhine, and Seine rivers and the canal network by the Belgian border around Lille. The busiest ports along the waterways are Paris, Strasbourg, and Rouen.

France's most important seaports are Marseille and Le Havre, which handle both passengers and freight. The busiest passenger ports are Calais and Boulogne, which have frequent services to England.

Air transportation is important. France is a focal point for international air traffic in Europe. Most international flights land at the Orly and Charles de Gaulle airports, just outside Paris. The latter handles more passengers than any other airport in Europe with the exception of London. Air France is the biggest of the three national airlines. UTA also operates international routes, while Air Inter provides passenger and extensive freight services within France.

Fact file : economy and trade

▽ **The distribution of French economic activity**

France was a mainly agricultural nation until the end of the nineteenth century. During the twentieth century, especially since the end of World War II, France has developed many industries. The main industrial areas are found around Paris, ports, and coalfields.

Key:	
	Shipbuilding
	Industry
	Mining
	Grapes and fruit
	Potatoes
	Sugar beet
	Fishing port
	Cattle
	Sheep
	Grain crops

Key Facts

Structure of production: Of the total GDP (the value of all economic activity in France), farming, forestry and fishing contribute 4 percent, industry 37 percent and services 59 percent.

Farming: *Main products:* barley, fruits, maize, milk, sugar beet, wheat, wine. *Livestock:* Cattle, 21,446,000; sheep, 11,490,000; goats, 1,236,000; pigs, 12,239,000; poultry, 213,000,000.

Mining: France is a major producer of high-grade iron ore. It also produces some bauxite, coal and lignite, and potash. Some oil is produced, mainly in the Landes region, but most oil is imported. Natural gas comes from the Lacq region, near the Pyrénées.

Energy: Of the total electrical energy produced in 1990, nuclear power stations contributed 70 percent, hydroelectric stations 18 percent, and power stations using coal, oil or gas 12 percent.

Manufacturing: France has aerospace, chemical, engineering, electrical and electronic, fashion, shipbuilding, steel, arms, and textile industries.

Economic growth: The average growth rate of France's gross national product (1980–91) was 1.8 percent per year.

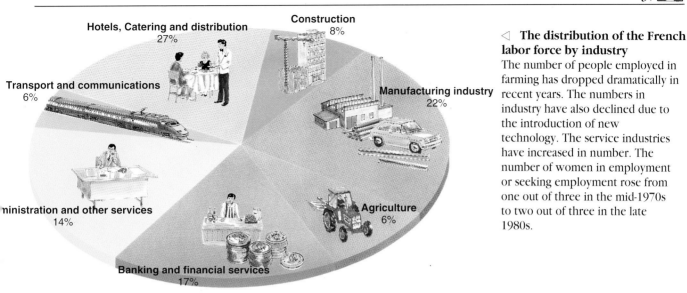

Hotels, Catering and distribution
27%

Construction
8%

Transport and communications
6%

Manufacturing industry
22%

Administration and other services
14%

Agriculture
6%

Banking and financial services
17%

◁ **The distribution of the French labor force by industry**
The number of people employed in farming has dropped dramatically in recent years. The numbers in industry have also declined due to the introduction of new technology. The service industries have increased in number. The number of women in employment or seeking employment rose from one out of three in the mid-1970s to two out of three in the late 1980s.

▷ **France's main trading partners in 1990**
France is one of the founder members of the European Community and EC countries accounted for more than half of France's external trade in the early 1990s. However, France continues to find other markets for its goods outside the EC.

French Exports

French Imports

(in billions of U.S. dollars)

Benelux
33.0   34.0

Germany (West)
37.8   45.9

UK
20.8   17.7

USA
13.4   19.8

Former USSR
1.6   3.5

Italy
25   28.2

Saudi Arabia
1.4   3.0

Rest of world
86.7   91.6

▽ **The composition of French imports and exports**
French imports are dominated by its need to import many raw materials, especially oil. France is trying to lessen its dependence on oil by developing nuclear power and other alternative sources.

Imports | Exports

Food and drink
11 | 15

Raw materials
21 | 23

Fuels
31 | 4

Manufactures
29 | 30

Services
23 | 21

(in billions of U.S. dollars)

Education

All French children must attend school between the ages of six and sixteen. Compulsory, free education has been provided by the government for more than a hundred years. Changes have occurred, but the main characteristics of French education remain the same today. In 1989–90 there were almost 2 million pupils in French primary and secondary schools.

The educational system is run by the government, which sets the curriculums and organizes nationwide examination. About 85 percent of the children attend schools run by the government. Private schools are mostly run by the Roman Catholic Church.

French schools offer a high standard of education and are very competitive. Children have to study a wide range of subjects until their final examinations. They must take written and oral tests during each school year before they move to the next class. There are fewer after-school activities than in many other countries.

Above: A mid-morning break at a large French primary school in Ivry, near Paris.

Below: A class in a French primary school can be quite formal, with little individual activity.

Before starting compulsory schooling, most French children attend a nursery school. During their five years at primary school, from the age of six, they are taught reading, writing, arithmetic, and learning skills.

The school day usually begins at 8 A.M., lunch is between noon and 2 P.M., and lessons end at 4 P.M. Wednesday is a free day but pupils must attend on Saturday morning.

At the age of eleven, the children transfer for four years to a *collège* for the first part of their secondary education. The most successful pupils then spend three years at a general *lycée* studying for the *baccalauréat* qualification. Others go to a vocational *lycée*, which trains them for working life.

Young people with a *baccalauréat* are entitled to free higher education at a university. Many of the best secondary school students go instead to a *grande école*. These famous colleges prepare students for top careers in business and government service.

Above: A class in a Roman Catholic school. Parents have the right to send their children to such private schools.

Below: The Sorbonne, in Paris, is a very famous university. It was founded in the thirteenth century.

The arts

French culture has given the world many great masterpieces in all fields of the arts. The oldest and most impressive achievements are the many great medieval cathedrals, such as those at Reims and Chartres. There are also fine palaces, including Versailles, built for King Louis XIV, and lovely *châteaux*, or mansions, along the Loire valley.

France's best-known painters were probably the Impressionists, who tried to show the changing effects of light. Among them were Pierre Auguste Renoir (1841-1919) and Claude Monet (1840-1926). The most famous French sculptor, Auguste Rodin (1840-1917), created such well-known works as *The Thinker.*

France also produced many outstanding figures in the field of music. Famous French composers include Hector Berlioz (1803-69), who wrote the *Symphonie Fantastique*; Claude Debussy (1862-1918), the composer of *Clair de Lune*; and Maurice Ravel (1875-1937), whose *Bolero* is world famous. France's best-known opera is *Carmen* by Georges Bizet (1838-75).

Above: The beautiful Cathedral of Notre Dame, in Paris, was built over seven hundred years ago.

Below: The *château* of Chambord is one of many fine palaces built along the Loire River.

Above: *The Luncheon of the Boating Party*, 1881, is a famous painting by Pierre Auguste Renoir, a founder member of the Impressionist group.

Below: Victor Hugo was not only a great novelist but also one of the leading French poets. His death in 1885 was mourned by the whole nation.

French literature has had a particularly important influence on politics, religion, and philosophy. Victor Hugo (1802-85), who wrote *The Hunchback of Notre-Dame*, dealt with the social issues of his time. Other great nineteenth-century novelists include Honoré de Balzac (1799-1850) and Emile Zola (1840-1902). In the twentieth-century Marcel Proust (1871-1922) is considered to be the finest French writer, author of the huge novel *Remembrance of Things Past.*

Since the 1890s many great French film directors and outstanding actors have together created masterpieces for the cinema. Among the finest directors were Jean Renoir (1894-1979), Jean Cocteau (1889-1963), and François Truffaut (1932-84), one of the most prominent of the recent French film makers.

In 1959 a ministry of culture was established to preserve France's rich cultural heritage, and make it more widely available outside Paris to encourage artistic creation. The government gives much financial aid to the arts.

The making of modern France

The boundaries of the modern state of France were established by about 1500. During the reign of Louis XIV (1643–1715) France became a very powerful nation and the arts flourished. After Louis XIV died, France's power declined, with a series of weaker kings who failed to understand the desires of the French people.

Increasingly social and economic problems led to calls for reforms in the system of government. Ideas on liberty and equality were promoted in the writings of such eighteenth-century thinkers as Voltaire and Jean-Jacques Rousseau. In 1789 a mob stormed the Bastille prison in Paris, and the Revolution began. France became a republic for the first time in 1792 and the king, Louis XVI, and his wife, Marie Antoinette, were executed. The new system only led to dictatorship and more discontent.

In 1799 a popular young general, Napoleon Bonaparte, seized power and five years later crowned himself emperor. He waged great military campaigns across Europe but was finally defeated at the battle of Waterloo, in Belgium in 1815, and exiled.

Above: Louis XIV in his coronation robes.
Left: The execution of Louis XVI in 1793.

Below: Napoleon, as Emperor of France, at the head of his "Great Army," which conquered Europe.

Left: A trench on the Verdun battlefront in World War I. About 450,000 French troops were killed here in 1916.

Above: German troops enter Paris in 1940.

Below: De Gaulle returns to Paris in August 1944.

During the rest of the nineteenth century France was ruled by a series of unstable regimes which failed to provide effective leadership. The nation gained many overseas possessions but was unable to rival the growing industrial and military might of other nations such as Britain and Germany. A disastrous defeat was suffered at the hands of a German army in 1871.

During the twentieth century France again had to face German aggression. In World War I (1914-18) France had greater losses of men than any other country. France was ill-prepared for the next invasion by Germany in 1940 and was easily defeated.

French resistance to the German occupation inside and from outside France was led by General Charles de Gaulle. After the war he became the dominant figure in French political life. He was President from 1944-46 but resigned, as he thought the system of government was too weak.

France in the modern world

During World War II France lost 80 percent of its factories, machinery, and means of transportation. By 1960 French production was double that of prewar years and had a growth rate second only to Japan among the industrial nations. France became a founder member of the European Economic Community in 1957. This powerful recovery took place despite a series of weak governments from 1945 to 1958 which struggled with rising prices and the conflicts in the countries of the French Empire. The Algerian revolt in 1958 brought a call for a new system of government.

The foundation of the Fifth Republic in 1958 by Charles de Gaulle began a new era in which France began to show a greater independence in world affairs.

De Gaulle took France out of NATO (the North Atlantic Treaty Organization), created France's own nuclear weapons, and began plans to modernize industry.

The end of de Gaulle's rule in 1969 began with strikes and disturbances during the spring of 1968, when demands were made for social, economic, and political reforms.

Left: France maintains defense agreements with several African countries and troops have been involved in peace-keeping in the Middle East.

Above: President de Gaulle speaks to the nation.
Below: Student riots and demonstrations occurred in 1968 as President de Gaulle's popularity fell.

Above: Farmers protest against the importation of cheap British meat in 1979. French farmers have generally gained much from the EEC agriculture policies.
Left: The Ariane rocket is an impressive symbol of French technology.

Below: President Mitterrand, who was elected in 1981 and again in 1988, addressed the British Houses of Parliament in 1984. He has visited many countries to present the French viewpoint on world affairs.

French economic growth received a major setback in 1973, when world oil prices rose steeply. A period of austerity was introduced to combat inflation and rising unemployment especially among the young. In the hope of a change, the first socialist government of the Fifth Republic, led by President François Mitterand, was elected in 1981. The new government nationalized some industries and banks and improved working conditions. Despite such changes, France still faces high unemployment and many economic problems. In the late 1980s the government was forced to change some of its policies.

France, however, remains one of the world's most powerful industrial and agricultural nations. France is likely to continue its independent policies in international affairs and maintain its leading role in the European Community.

Fact file : government and world role

Key Facts

Official name: *République Française* (French Republic).

Flag: The Tricolor.

National anthem: *La Marseillaise*, written by C. Rouget de Lisle in 1792.

National government: *Head of State*: The President,. Elected by direct universal suffrage for a seven-year term. A nine-member Constitutional Council ensures that the President's election is fair. The President appoints the Prime Minister who, with the Council of Ministers, directs the operation of the government. *Parliament*: Parliament consists of the directly elected National Assembly, containing 577 Deputies, and the 319-member Senate, which is elected indirectly.

Local government: France is divided into twenty-two regions for planning and financial matters. Within the twenty-two regions are ninety-six *départements*, which are governed by an elected *Conseil General*. France also has small local government units, called *communes*. Most *communes* have less than 1,500 inhabitants, but they are run by elected Municipal Councils, headed by a mayor. The five Overseas Departments are governed by an appointed Commissioner and an elected *Conseil General.*

Defense: *Army*: The strength of the Army in 1992 was 260,900. There is compulsory military service for twelve months, but people may choose alternative work, such as in civil defense or in former French overseas territories. *Navy*: 64,900 (1989), *Air Force*: 91,700 (1990).

Economic alliances: France was one of the six founder members of the European Economic Community (or Common Market) in 1957. The EEC is now the world's largest trading bloc.

Political alliances: France is a member of the UN and the Council of Europe. It withdrew from the North Atlantic Treaty Organization (NATO) in 1966, but it remained a member of the Atlantic Alliance.

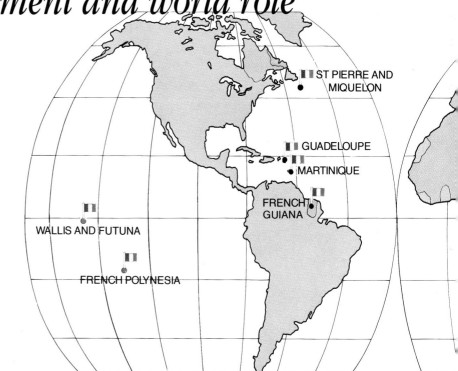

The President is the supreme authority of the French Republic and has great power. He can dismiss the Prime Minister and dissolve the National Assembly. He makes the most important decisions which are confirmed by the Council of Ministers. He is head of the Armed Forces and he alone can authorize the use of nuclear weapons.

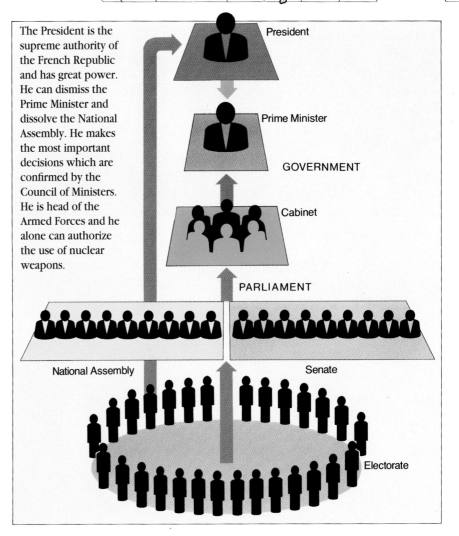

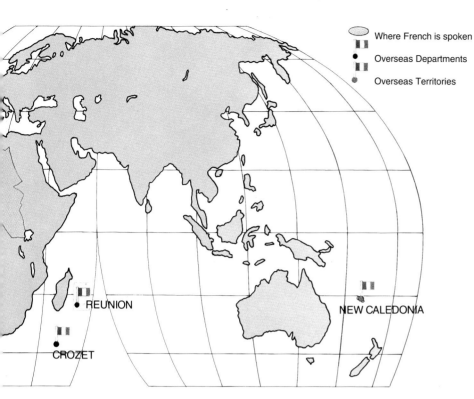

Where French is spoken
Overseas Departments
Overseas Territories

REUNION

CROZET

NEW CALEDONIA

◁ The French influence
France has had two large empires—in North America and Africa. The French language is still spoken in many of its former colonies.

◁ French overseas possessions
Today France retains only a few small possessions scattered throughout the world. Overseas departments are regarded as a part of France while territories have more independence.

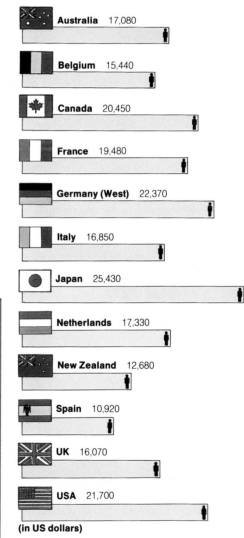

Australia 17,080
Belgium 15,440
Canada 20,450
France 19,480
Germany (West) 22,370
Italy 16,850
Japan 25,430
Netherlands 17,330
New Zealand 12,680
Spain 10,920
UK 16,070
USA 21,700

(in US dollars)

△ National wealth created per person in 1990
France has one of the world's largest economies. Its people have one of the world's highest standards of living. Technical progress and high productivity have enabled France to continue to be a wealthy nation.

▽ The European Community
There are now twelve member countries of the European Community. The aims of the Community are to bring a closer union between the peoples of Europe and to provide economic expansion. Many trade barriers have been abolished between members, there are common policies for agriculture and fisheries. Workers can now move more freely within the Community. Decisions are taken by a Council of Ministers. A European Parliament, first elected in 1979, debates all policy issues put forward by the Council.

IRELAND
UNITED KINGDOM
DENMARK
NETHERLANDS
BELGIUM
GERMANY
LUXEMBOURG
FRANCE
ITALY
PORTUGAL
SPAIN
GREECE

Index

PRINTED IN BELGIUM BY

INTERNATIONAL BOOK PRODUCTION

DATE DUE

MAY 0 5 2004			